DRUM
Class Method

by Alyn J. Heim

FORWORD

This is a method for the drum class. It effectively presents the rudiments of drumming and the reading of music in a manner and at a pace designed to accommodate the specific needs of group instruction.

Each technique or rudiment is introduced by a rote <u>Drill</u>, developed through a reading <u>Exercise</u>, and refined by a <u>Solo</u> performance that stimulates interest and challenges each member of the group.

This new method contains fresh ideas that will be welcomed by the class drum teacher. In Book I the "free-bounce" approach to rolls is introduced and developed with explanations to both teacher and student. A full section is devoted to six-eight time using a method that enables the student to learn the rhythm "in-two" from the beginning. Book II begins with sixteenth notes and progresses to some of the more advanced rudiments and reading material. More than half of each book is devoted to appealing solo material which is designed to develop the student by encouraging enthusiastic practice.

About the author: Dr. Heim received his Bachelor of Science degree from the Juilliard School of Music where he majored in tympani and percussion under Saul Goodman. His Master of Arts degree in Music Education was earned at Columbia Teachers College, and his Doctorate in Music Education at New York University. He is a former member of the Houston Symphony Orchestra and a music teacher and supervisor in the public schools of New Jersey.

2

$\frac{2}{4}$ Time

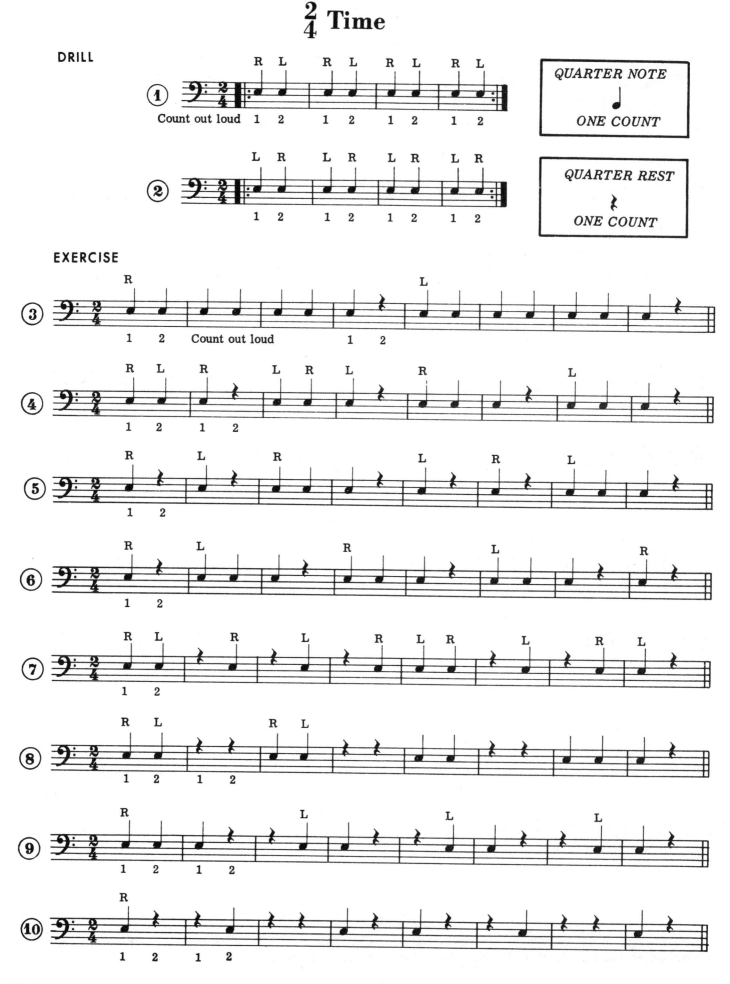

Solo Page

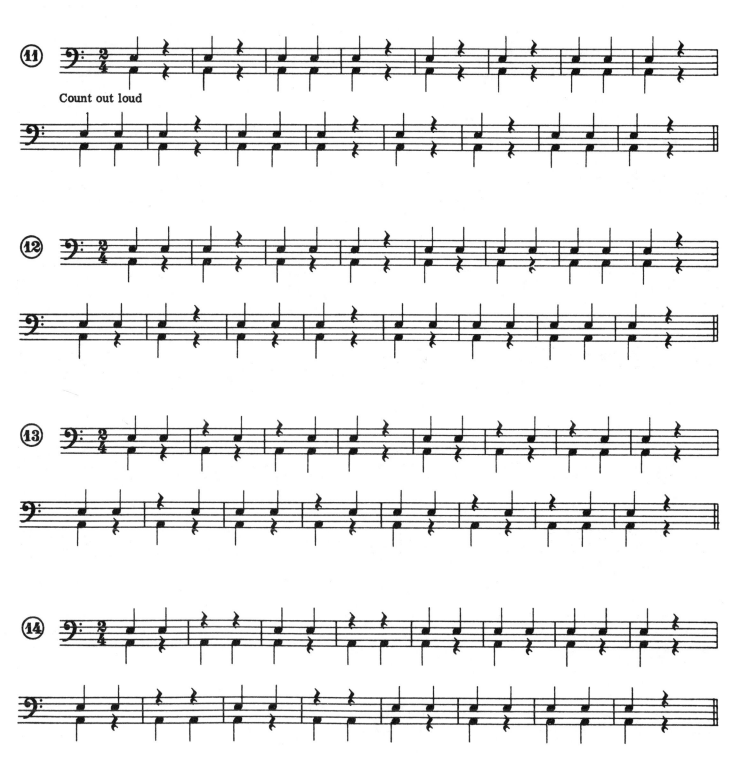

Count out loud

Class can be divided into snare drum and bass drum players. Students with sufficient coordination should be encouraged to play the bass drum part with the right foot.

E. L. 1335

$\frac{4}{4}$ Time

Solo Page

SNARE DRUM
BASS DRUM

⑪

Count out loud

⑫

⑬

⑭

$\frac{3}{4}$ Time

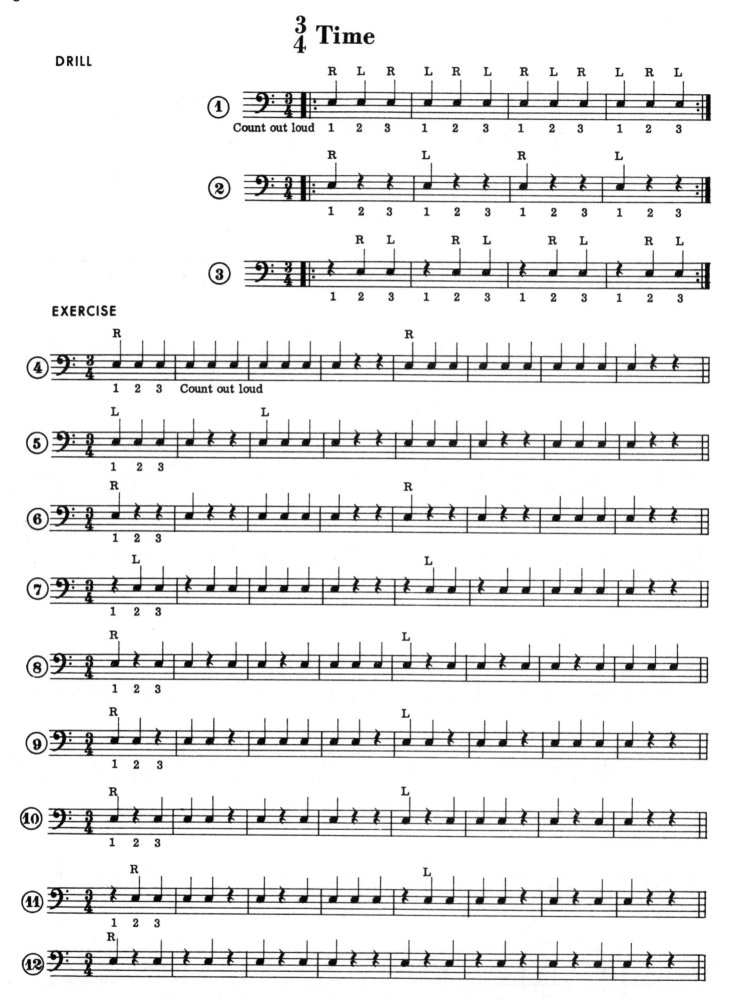

Solo Page

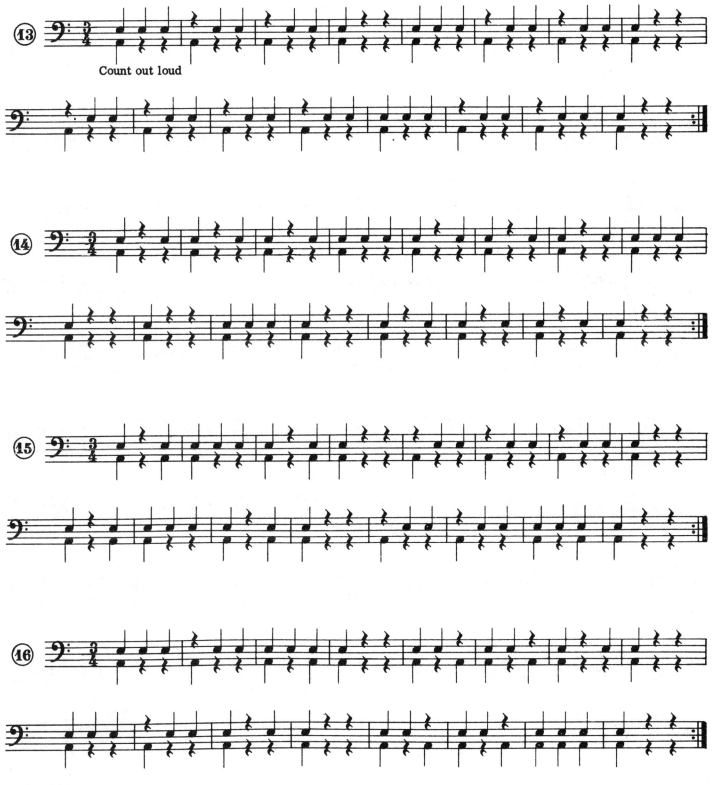

Eighth Notes

E. L. 1335

Solo Page

Divide the class into snare drum and bass drum players. Use some students on real instruments for the sound. Well-coordinated students should play the bass drum part with their right foot.

E. L. 1335

The Roll (to the teacher)

The traditional approach to teaching rolls has been to begin with a double stroke on each hand.

This is gradually speeded up until the double stroke becomes a bounce.

Eventually the double bounce is developed to a speed fast enough to sound like a roll.

This method is very slow and often not successful in developing a good closed roll. Most professional drummers use a multiple bounce and not a double for a closed roll. This free bounce contains more than two bounces on each stroke. This technique gives the professional roll the closed sound that the student roll often lacks. At the same given tempo the multiple bounce will sound closed while the double bounce will sound open.

This professional technique may seem difficult to develop yet it is more simple and practical than the standard approach. The demonstrations on the following page will illustrate how a student can perform a multiple bounce immediately. This free bounce becomes a closed roll at almost the first attempt, and the student is on his way to refining his roll to quality. These results are in sharp contrast to the length of time the double stroke method consumes.

The roll exercises in this book can be used with either the double or multiple bounce method. The explanations refer to the multiple bounce technique but can easily be applied to the traditional double stroke.

E. L. 1335

The Bounce Stroke
(roll preparation)

A stick that is allowed to drop freely will bounce a number of times before coming to rest on the drum or pad. This principle can be illustrated by the following demonstration:

1. Touch the tip of the left stick to the drum or pad. Holding this left wrist still, lift the tip of the stick with the right hand. When the stick is released it will bounce four or five times before coming to rest. Do the same experiment with the right hand.

LEFT HAND BOUNCE

RIGHT HAND BOUNCE

The <u>Traditional Grip</u> is pictured for the left hand

If the <u>Matched Grip</u> is preferred, both hands would hold the stick as pictured for the right hand.

The amount of pressure at point "A" will determine the speed of the bounce (more pressure, faster bounce - less pressure, slower bounce).

2. Now we produce the bounce without the aid of our free hand. Starting with our stick in a raised position, we turn our wrist in the same way as for a normal down stroke. When the stick strikes the drum or pad we leave our wrist in this low position, allowing the stick to bounce.

3. The last, and very important, step is lifting the stick off the drum or pad before the bounce has stopped. The stick should be held in the low position long enough to bounce but not long enough to come to rest. The number of bounces can be accurately controlled by lifting at the proper time. The number of bounces need not be counted at this stage, all that is necessary now is being sure that the stick is lifted before coming to rest. If it is allowed to rest on the drum or pad at the end of the bounce a "crushed" sound will develop in the roll.

The following exercises will help develop this bounce and lift technique.

IMPORTANT: Before going on to the next page, the eighth note studies (pages 8 and 9) should now be practiced again, this time with the student playing a bounce stroke for each eighth note.

Five Stroke Roll

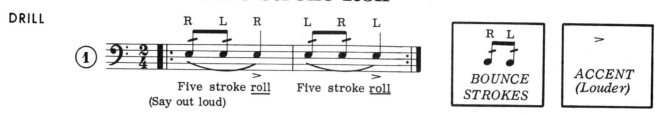

DRILL

The rudiment name should be said out loud before doing this drill. The rhythm of the words can easily be imitated by the students after the teacher has said them in tempo a few times. In this way the rhythm of the rudiment is supplied by the rhythm of the words and the student associates the rudiment sound with the sound of its name.

The rudiment name should also be said out loud while being played, and the word roll can be said louder to help the hands accent that stroke.

EXERCISE

Solo Page

Nine Stroke Roll

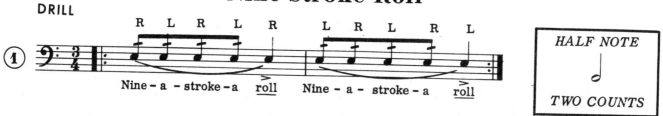

DRILL

The rudiment name with the added syllables should be said out loud.

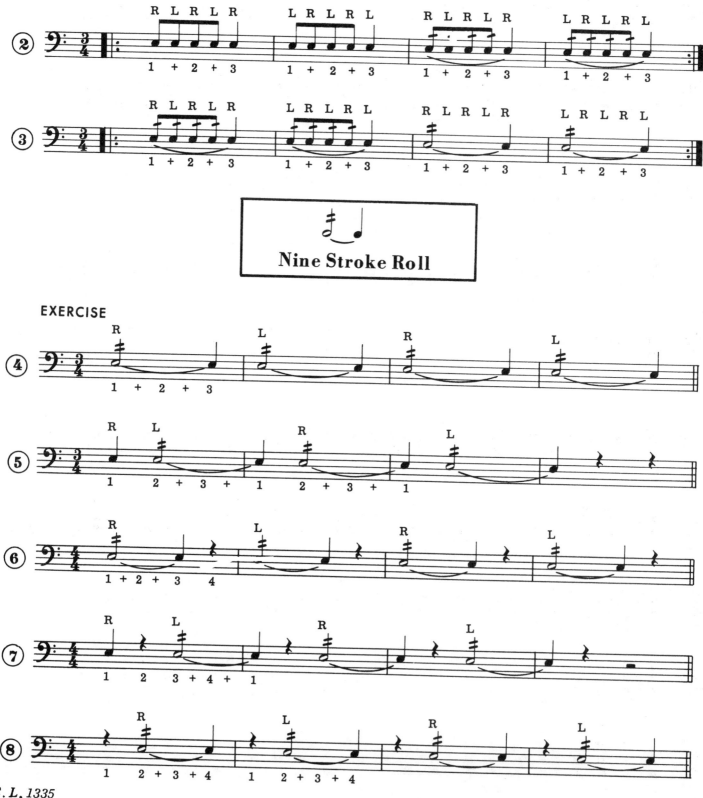

Solo Page
5 & 9 Stroke Rolls

Flams

A flam is played by striking both sticks at almost the same time. Stick position is the important factor in playing flams correctly.

LEFT HAND FLAM

RIGHT HAND FLAM

If both strokes start at the same time the low stick will strike first. Due to the height the second stroke will sound louder. The flam is named Right or Left for this second, louder stroke.

DRILL

As the rudiment speeds up the word is shortened from fa-lam to flam.

EXERCISE

Flams are usually played hand to hand, however since flams with the same hand are easier to play they are introduced first. At very fast tempos, even the well schooled drummer will find flams with the same hand more natural and effective.

E. L. 1335

Alternating Flams
(Hand to Hand)

DRILL

EXERCISE

IMPORTANT: For additional flam practice the quarter note solos (pages 3, 5, 7) should now be played with flams for each note.

$\frac{2}{4}$ Flam Tap

DRILL

EXERCISE

IMPORTANT: For additional flam-tap study the eighth note solos (page 9) should now be played with a flam-tap for each two eighth notes and a flam for each quarter note.

E. L. 1335

Conclusion Solos-Section I
Military Street Beat

Drummer's Waltz

<u>Note:</u> Observe Dynamic markings for an effective performance.

The Parade March

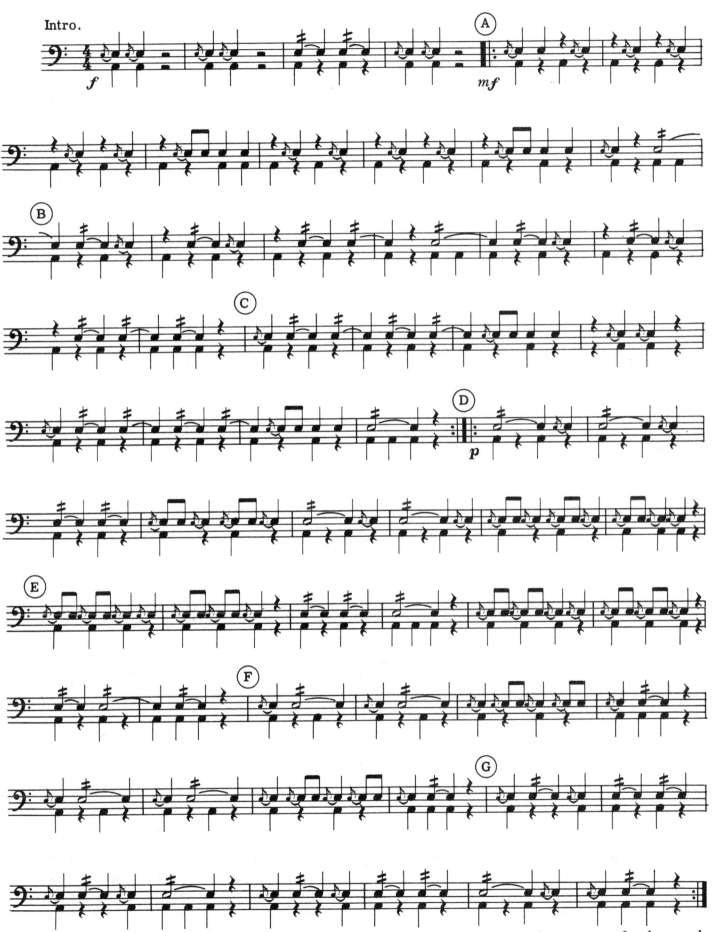

Divide the class into snare drum and bass drum players. Use some students on real instruments for the sound. Well-coordinated students should play the bass drum part with their right foot.

E. L. 1335

$\frac{6}{8}$ Time

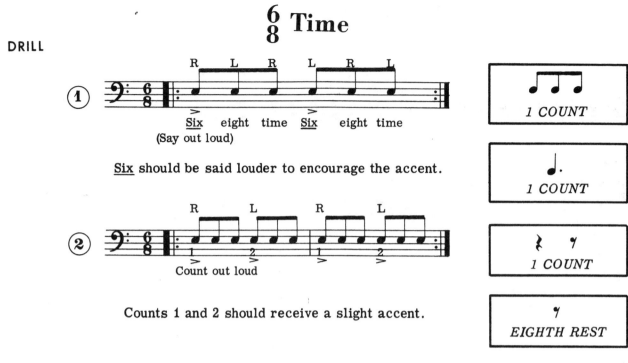

Six should be said louder to encourage the accent.

Counts 1 and 2 should receive a slight accent.

EXERCISE

Solo Page

$\frac{6}{8}$ Time(cont.)

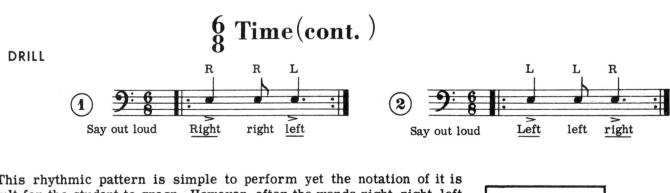

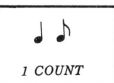

This rhythmic pattern is simple to perform yet the notation of it is difficult for the student to grasp. However, after the words right-right-left have been said in rhythm a few times by the teacher, the students easily imitate it. We take advantage of this by teaching the rhythm in "two" without asking the student, at this stage, to fully comprehend the exact notation.

EXERCISE

Solo Page

Seven Stroke Roll

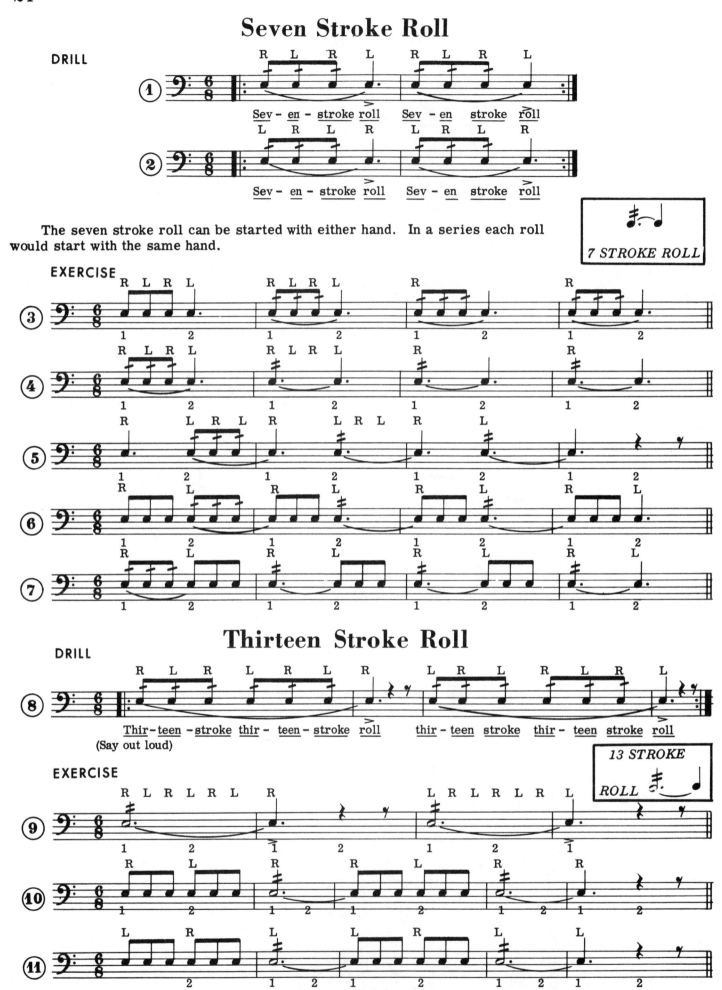

The seven stroke roll can be started with either hand. In a series each roll would start with the same hand.

Thirteen Stroke Roll

Solo Page
7 and 13 Stroke Rolls

$\frac{6}{8}$ Flam Tap

DRILL

IMPORTANT: For additional flam-tap study pages 22 and 23 should now be played using a flam-tap on each quarter and eighth note combination.

Flam Accent

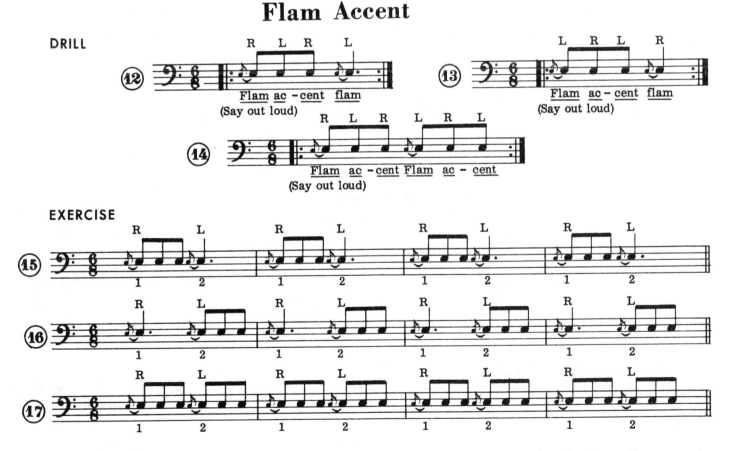

DRILL

EXERCISE

IMPORTANT: For additional flam accent study pages 20 and 21 should now be played using a flam accent on the eighth note groups. Page 26 should be played supplying flam-taps and flam accents.

E. L. 1335

Conclusion Solos-Section II

Bugle Beat

Echo Street Beat

The Rider's March

Divide the class into snare drum and bass drum players. Use some students on real instruments for the sound. Well-coordinated students should play the bass drum part with their right foot.

Duet For Two Snare Drums

March Time

The Challenge

Duet

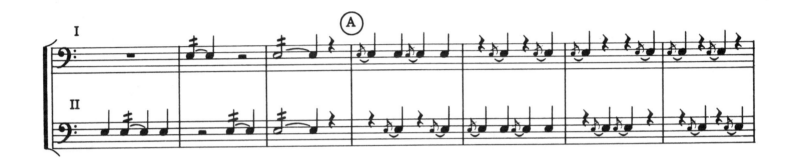

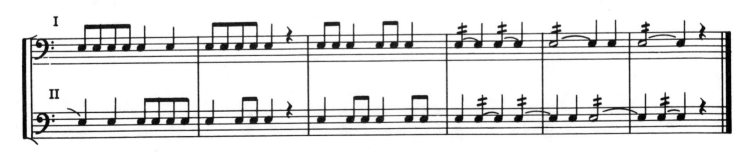

E. L. 1335